WHY ARE YOU SHOUTING?

James Womack lives in Cambridge, where he teaches Spanish and study skills. He is the author of three previous collections of poetry with Carcanet: *Misprint* (2012), *On Trust: A Book of Lies* (2017) and *Homunculus* (2020). He also translates widely from Spanish and Russian, most recently Camilo José Cela's *The Hive* (NYRB Classics, 2023).

WHY
ARE
YOU
SHOUTING?

JAMES
WOMACK

CARCANET POETRY

First published in Great Britain in 2024 by
Carcanet
Alliance House, 30 Cross Street
Manchester, M2 7AQ
www.carcanet.co.uk

ISBN 978 1 80017 453 5

Book design by Andrew Latimer, Carcanet
Typesetting by LiteBook Prepress Services
Printed in Great Britain by SRP Ltd, Exeter, Devon

The publisher acknowledges financial
assistance from Arts Council England.

CONTENTS

v

—Voici donc un syllogisme exemplaire. Le chat a quatre pattes. Isidore et Fricot ont chacun quatre pattes. Donc Isidore et Fricot sont chats.

—Mon chien aussi a quatre pattes.

—Alors, c'est un chat.

Eugène Ionesco, Rhinocéros

WHY ARE YOU SHOUTING?

I

THE CITY, AN ARGUMENT

I.

Beloved, the city curves as a sickle. Politicians have written rhapsodies to its impermanence, its occasional gross expansions. Month on month the city drags the sea close into its formal harbours and casual inlets. An odd kind of embrace followed soon after by predictable rejection. The walls do not yield.

Beloved, the city does not stay still. Where was wasteland a month ago now a suburb: uninhabited, pristine, bright. The arterial roads mirage from the sun. The direction of travel is not yet determined. Running to or running away. A liquid, it fills all available space. Alleyways writhe and cross.

Beloved, the city knows its worth. No traveller comes here but is informed of this fact. Chauvinism shades into a kind of weeping arrogance. Microcosm, every barrio believes itself better than the others. After the match each weekend there is always violence. This is not unusual. A boy is stabbed.

Beloved, the city is still a child. Incontinent, satisfied with a breast and a swaddled bed. Useless from labour. Useless for work. The city *does* nothing: it takes and grows. The city has your eyes. We look at the city with the love we cannot spare for our own children.

Beloved, the city is sexless. The ripe displays of our childhood have disappeared. A new louder kind of innocence. Mystics and stylites have a vocabulary we cannot coincide. Vows are asked of them. To flee in a desert the approach of mankind. The city asks no new vows of us.

Beloved, in a mirror the city confuses us. We never invited mirror trust. It seems a test of some kind. To have your own face given back to you upside-down. Your teeth where your windows should be. Roads instead of the tight squirms and curls of a more legitimate brain.

Beloved, the city wakes up after the weekend. The city is in the corner of your eye. You hope that some fragment of the dead days will survive. An abandoned high-heel shoe. An abandoned pint glass of shocking orange urine. Full of commuters an abandoned train passes over a bridge.

II.

Beloved, the city is nothing if not just. A single glance, the wrong word at the wrong time means honour must be satisfied. Duels, rapier or pistol, take place on the dusty backlots. When the city is called to join our larger wars, then all personal affronts are temporarily abandoned.

Beloved, the city splits and runs like a silver ball. Touched it does nothing other than yield, for all that we wish it to resist. In the harshest winters it moves sluggishly. In high summer it hurtles around like a mad thing, separating and resolving into grand bridges and towers.

Beloved, the city makes great claims for its intellect. Coupled with a certain moral flexibility, this has led to its current line of work. The machine works slowly but is always effective. Shipping movements are relayed to its superiors. Blood bubbles out and drips from the side of its head.

Beloved, the city feeds itself. It can nourish itself on perfumes—road tar and frying fish, the sweat and Chanel of summer—as well as the more recognisable steaks and garbage. Roles forced upon us. We are à la carte anatomists. This is not just food. It is unjust food.

Beloved, there are times when the city is generous. The tables spread to groaning. The mother runs unchallenged from the corner shop, her child both shield and excuse of the tins stashed under the pushchair. Pavements split with dandelions, purslane. Feast at the corner where dogs piss. Burdock and bedstraw.

Beloved, the city can never say it is sated. Ephemera we think we lose are never fully vanished. The scroll of a price tag picked off and rolled away. The playing cards spilled from a window. Flirtatious auto-destruct online messages. The city gathers it all, the city always wants more.

Beloved, the city shows its morning face. That noise the grim of adolescent complaint, the background hum of everything not being perfect. Shells and slime! Move it, move it! A step slower than our slowest participant. Industrial concrete suddenly an object of deep interest. The end of it an education.

III.

Beloved, a city for lovers. Lovers congregate at sites of least offensive photographic interest. Bridges collapse under the weight of padlocks. A single man cannot move from the hospital to the churchyard unless he elbow himself past crowds of the infatuated. Buses arrive daily on swift turnarounds. Open for business.

Beloved, the city is an undelivered city of messengers. News is borne from the northern hills to the curve of the central river, in the movement of an eye and the turn of a hand. All is information, messages transmitted and eternally received. A letter always arrives at its destination.

Beloved, your city is an angry city. Peevish even before the morning fog has been burned away, we notice the first signs in earbud executives, their wasp-sharp faces. One spark could set the Whole. Thing. Off. A man jostled at the wrong moment, a car changing lanes. Don't touch me!

Beloved, the city is a clamshell on the waves. There was land, and then there was hell, and then there was the eternal city. Born naked. It drives you mad, the city, that itch at the edge of your waking mind. No way but this. When desire fades, you weep.

Beloved, the city can restrain itself. Gourmet and not gourmand, we are invited to know the city as a set of experiences, of visits to the planetarium, the pumping station, the light on the sandy college walls, wondering if here, here will be a first kiss, a first brief declaration.

Beloved, this week's monster is the city. Baleen-mouthed, it battens on the excreta of its parasites, our abandoned residue, gorging itself on grease and turds, wet-wipes and condoms, slow water and the unbearable rush of the tunnel bore. You know this sick greed, the squabble to consume, vomit, consume again.

Beloved, the city eats and shits its citizens. One glorious morning! Our impedimenta tied in a handkerchief, stick slung over our shoulder, we arrive and see the skyline awaken before us in its watercolour gold. No illusion can hold this back: each tower is hard enamel, mouth whole, tongue river.

IV.

Beloved, the city is always upwards. Complaints no longer reach the tops of the tallest buildings. The skyline that so impressed our ancestors is seen now as prelude. The future tall, a ladder to the moon. Glass and steel hacked from the Welsh mines, dragged overland at immense human cost.

Beloved, the city blows a trumpet. Boots and saddles. Drop everything and prepare for war. There on the coast the enemy hordes, weapons concealed in torn canvas bags, their uniform ragged, their pockets empty, most of them dead. The survivors disguised as women and children. As expected, we shall resist.

Beloved, the city this morning looks cruel. Her lip a harsh slash of Rouge Diabolique, her eyes defined into oblivion. Sometimes one dresses to impress, sometimes one must dress to intimidate. Makeup is an environment. Even the clouds seem to catch themselves and redress. Even the clouds, even the rain.

Beloved, the city is a noted carouser. Drink so deep from the ramshorn that the seas sink and drowned villages rise above the waves. Eat so greedily that the plates themselves are consumed. Relax with one final sherry in the Senior Common Room, the World Serpent purring at your feet.

Beloved, the city is an ant-nest miracle. From the gritted outyards to the nucleus, that black hole which drags everything—mostly money—into its orbit, each eusocial part seems to work for the good of the whole. What a fine place to sink into, one might think, sinking irreparably in.

Beloved, there are no other cities. None at least that compare with this one. The hamlets and hovels which surround us can only dream of their submission or incorporation. The height of yearning, to be one day suburbia. Parkway. Golf course. What we are owed is only what we deserve.

Beloved, there is no way to look directly at the city. Spend too long with your eyes open, and you will no longer see colours. All will fade to a forgetful grey, and the soft faces of those who walk towards you will seem indeterminate, the faces of the dead.

V.

Beloved, the city just wants to be touched, or believes it wants to be touched. Although, if it is touched, the slightest contact will snail it back into its home. It is easy to offend the city. Imagined slights become vast bubbles. I thought you were such a good friend.

Beloved, the city has been caught *in flagrante*, its dick in the pie. You can understand the temptation, but such invitations should be resisted. The chiselled boulevards, the air and delicacy of the parks, all swaying together in a single inescapable net. The rest of the pantheon invited to mock.

Beloved, is the city implacable? Are we no more than some great Bedlam, where our crimes are on display alongside our foibles, and the gross public uses us as a Sunday afternoon excursion? Is the Casa Mila a source of innocent merriment? Is there balance, or justice? Is there sickness?

Beloved, the city invites us to pursue her, right to the doors of her many bedchambers. A question, in this brave world of questions: when is the right moment to abandon the chase? Our deserts, the gratification of these desires—the city turns to us and never seems so beautiful.

Beloved, the city knows empathy can be fatal. Is there anything worse than the way certain stories end? I know what you're going through. Come, sit next to me. Poor child. There is manipulation in the city's kindness, just as there can be a degree of innocence in her anger.

Beloved, the city reaches into the ricebowl with almost delicate fingers. Sorts the grain from the maggots, divides what will be left from what is to be consumed. A handful of that writhing protein, that gives you soul in your mouth. Void heart. King soul. Our customs are not yours.

Beloved, the end of the city is upon us. The sharp shadow decadence that overcomes her every seven days. 'This is a kind of marriage', we once thought, equating partnership with surrender. A two days' wonder. The blurred head of the morning after; the life of the world to come.

VI.

Beloved, the city only sometimes hurries to life. Crowds gather like sunspots at the naos. A hundred myriad people, men and boys, follow the swings and cycles. I lived close to this temple once, and could hear nothing from my lover's shuttered window. This does not mean that nothing happened.

Beloved, the city low-key flicks v-signs at hearses. A family of ten children is common and supported by the state. Everyone will live forever is the general tenor of things. The Year Six Parents WhatsApp group is the place to hunt for resources: flat-front grey cotton trousers; a solid-state orthicon.

Beloved, the city doesn't want to hear this. Furious mothers calling their children home in the mid-afternoon, the siesta ruptured, the panic setting in to their voices. All the children hurried in from the streets, the parks left in the burning sun, an ice-cream van calling uselessly across the tarmac.

Beloved, in the hills around the city a storm has flourished for the past three and a half centuries. Travellers speak of dust clouds and an intense suffocating heat, something under the ground that groans and curses. A space of withered trees and abandoned settlements it is impolite to discuss.

Beloved, the city is a trapdoor spider. That tribe which Walckenaer has named *vagrants*. From a little cell formed of the rolled up leaf of a plant, it darts upon any insect which happens to pass. The city and its affinities conceal themselves in a long cylindrical straight silken tube.

Beloved, there is a knock at the city gate. Feet shuffle toward the barred wooden wicket. The peephole—it is late at night—swings open, with a faint yellow light behind it. The lockkeeper voice that asks your business is querulous, ancient. For an old man to have such power.

Beloved, the city is hungry, hungry beyond need. It eats what it wants, and whatever it does not want. Touch it: the city will have you in its mouth forever. You are not entrapped to your return: instead—all the better to eat you with—it's love that calls you.

VII.

Beloved, the city will do nothing. I passed one of its gardens, and saw the wild roses grow, the thorn and the unkempt thistle spread and stretch. It tells you its dreams, and talks of food and drink: an animal life. Laziness by what authority? The city has no scripture.

Beloved, the city opens and breathes. You can say to yourself *Well I give what I give*; the relationship is always uneven. Saints and ascetics are donors above us, but net recipients even they. Six o'clock in the afternoon approaches: what have we done to earn this calm, these bells?

Beloved, the city has been petulant, has soldiered, has set itself above us all. And what of it? Now she is small and new-unknowledged, curled asleep on a beanbag. Her face has relaxed into the speaking mask of all children; as a mind builds behind it, and all we owe.

Beloved, the city invites us to this square. Walk the length of one side: the sheltered one. Perfumeries and sweet shops. Quarter turn. Walk, *pausadamente*. Quarter turn. Walk, exhaling. High-end boutiques and hat stalls. Quarter turn. *Pausadamente*, again. You are both where you began, and five hundred yards further on.

Beloved, the city of all things is the smallest. A nothing in permanent harsh light. To look at, barely more than a grain, subdued and uncommunicative. The Tsar once offered a prize to anyone who could measure the city, a prize which remained unclaimed at the time of his death.

Beloved, there remains one barrier to victory over the city. Anti-climb paint and cacti spikes. Every day more people make the attempt. I saw wounds to hands and feet, the side, the head. I saw one arm, skin split like a torsioning weisswurst; its owner a mute and dazed fourteen-year-old.

Beloved, there is a softening in the city. Grey hair forms rings around her head, around his head (for what pronouns the city has!). This skin has survived intact, and is now soft as shammy-leather. Strange and expensive ointments, applied daily, over the course of several lustra. You may touch.

VIII.

Tenella! Tenella! Tenella!
Tenella! Tenella! Tenella!

Beloved, the city is mine now. That throb at the back of your head—my feet, dancing. Let us not say I come from the east, the south: let us instead say only I am here from *elsewhere*. But you know me, do you not? Cousin, you do know me?

II

test results are in
call me when you get a chance
(and the hurricane)

ULYANOVSK, A LETTER

a.

I saw the city in a dream. I rode a train
of polished red wood. I recognised the fallen
statues of the gods, their smooth dispassionate faces
half-buried in the river mud. Any country,
looked at longer than a second, is not quite sane.

In real life, I sat at an occasional table
and wrote in jewelled black ink, hour after slow hour,
my impressions of the city. My roommate asked
who are you writing to? and my unthought reply,
I don't know, was deemed acceptable.

I also sat in dive bars, sadly saying *hit me*
and taking my punishment like a man.
This? It's my emotional support vodka.
No one thought this entitled, or odd:
a country where the king can say *L'état, it me.*

You could write a small history of any war
in pictures of men who look up from their work
at the cavalry riding past. All human life is life
glimpsed from a field—dogweed and rusting iron,
unstoppable parched grass, poppy and madder.

The houses and roads have lost their mission.
Tonight is a hot country. I would like to sit
in a cool restaurant in a hot country,
about to be brought a plate of white fish.
I slump against the bar in the sleep of reason.

b.

I'm going to steal a bit of your life, do you mind?
A touch of its honey? We are the children of excess,
as though money could breed like an animal.
We are all in this together, they said.
I said *No, we are all in this alone.*

And I sat by the river and heard the barges pass
with a slow whale-song of longing at dusk.
I have not tried to write an innocent history:
if you pity me, tell me where I can go to think.
How could you be Russian, somewhere else?

After the second bottle: *Is a snailshell a maze?*
What price your marrow, and what price your sleep?
How many people believe what they are saying?
Questions and only an occasional answer:
The song the Sirens sang was not the Marseillaise.

I show my dreams to myself in the early morning.
The bedroom is negative cinema—
a blackout curtain with light at the edges.
Orpheus composes his wife; death turns us into words,
but the flesh calls, unhurriedly calls for something.

Why dispute it, if a dream adds to your enjoyment?
They told us they had been into the sky
and looked around and seen no trace of God.
I laughed, because they did not know the sky is God.
I wish my Lord was a mountain lion.

C.

The blossom viral on the cherry trees.
Last night we had a thunderstorm in style
across the river, a ghastly calm on our side.
My life seems a single detail withheld,
that flows indifferent. *Je pense pas, donc je suis.*

Even the sea repents, but a river, never.
The language has grown out of me.
The five emotions are happiness, sadness, anger, sadness, revenge.
I'm not in the same town you were born in
and I thought you wanted to break, no replies to my letter.

By the time you read these words, everything is worse:
you are only saints so much as you wish to be.
I walked the boundaries, pulling a human splinter
from the retail subconscious of the world:
not the marketplace, but the planned economy of ideas.

Yellow-grey, brownish light of a night-time study.
I only get to write to you when England is on the way
to midnight, and a single confused little beetle
crawls around on my desk. Lie still,
for I must anatomise you, great city.

'What are all these flowers for?'
                                        'Oh, sorry, you are dead.'
City, I will pass through your life and be forgotten.
like buildings stand while history speeds around them.
A city with a long history of rejecting itself
vs. a river-stone, smooth as a baby's forehead.

What will you do now? I'm off to create prophecies.
Large fish hang still in clear water;
the tragic commons share in the sunlight.
I tap the microphone and say *Is this thing on?*
I close my eyes and see the rain falling into place.

CHANGE PLUS VITE, HÉLAS ...

Back in the city after years away
here I am, motherfuckers, putting Baudelaire to the test,
ready to slot back in, if anyone will have me ...
Oy, the pavements have twisted in my memory
and nothing here loves me as you loved me.

I used to lust for the laidoutness of it all:
brick on brick, soul on soul, supermarket poetry.
The swive-tired past, glass over ruins;
this present a permanent hectic free-fall,
screwed together by advertising hoardings.

Adios to God! This blue tarmac one huge yawn
indifferent and | or unhappy, but never mine.
The maps have changed, the names have no streets,
the buildings die, the vapour lights are born.
Skol a glass to it all, though there is no peace.

Your city now is not your city then is not
her city ever is not the city that you shared:
what language did she even sigh in?
You'll never remember; the past is variglot,
and there's no language once we make it to Zion.

Guau guau, gav gav, hau hau, bow wow:
the dogs tell their truth in palimpsest,
and a needle-blind finch sings all the more sweetly.
For now, my promises are placed in escrow.
Every kiss, your kiss, is the kiss that got away.

pink cherry blossom
in fresh fallen may snow

it is nothing nothing
the almanac is useless

SEASONS

I.

The city is dead, and yes, the country too,
and probably, beyond, the grey wide world.
Dead without the brakes on, moving forwards,
unaware of status-change, pathetic and hopeful.
We have no tocsin to unsettle the dead
whom their directors have prepared for everything.

There are five vowels, and six or seven continents:
most of what has happened
or will shortly happen is inevitable,
and evil calls out OOOO, or is that just the blood in my temples.
When evil occurs there are always omens:
even the lightning strike, the swift wrath of God, was prefigured
and evil calls out OOOO, and there is blood in the temples.

Back when I was a teacher, a Chinese student politely
asked questions of his online dictionary,
which suddenly said the word 'delusion' in a bland female voice.
The city is dead, cry it to no one:
my life is that single detail withheld.

January blossoms, the ice-cream parlours crammed on Boxing Day.
Another student sent me a photograph, herself as the snow fell,
joy to her face at the white flies in the air.
And when we spoke a few days later, it was all melted,
the mercury hovered at the cusp of nothing.

II.

Kidnapped Helen calls for maps, statistics:
Show me the benefits of the war:
what does it help us to open the African markets?
It can't all have been because of this face—
who goes to war for beauty?
Is love, or beauty, any kind of justification?

One day, I thought, she will go out and not come back.
Orgasms bombard us. Autumn me, life!
Give me fruitfulness, though it's clear what awaits.
Let it all turn to fire under my hands.
What is orgasm like? Orgasm is what happens
if the body attains the limit of its capacities,
and then for a second surpasses it.
It is having your palm cupped against a smooth clay bowl
that is filled with boiling water,
the heat gradually touching your flesh,
comfort, then fright.
The world has died while I slept, and slept while I died.
At morning the moths all light out for the sun.

I lived in a jungle, sticky with thunderbugs,
a storm promised and never delivered,
rain no more than warm spit.
I performed as I had been asked to,
built gothic work in a sweltering world;
we spoke about this, in the rutted sheets.

She says that love is located in the solar plexus,
just below the ribs … *Here, here is where the wall breaks down.*
Pressure, slight hurt, building against my eyes.
Myth is useless: when someone tells you the same story twice,

it means they don't care about you.
I have seen the statue of Memnon at Thebes,
standing out in the solitude of a barley field.

III.

New generation, you arrived after it all happened.
You have missed something—
the bird-feeder swings wild on a windless day.
You are all still polite, with no reason:
my son talks in his sleep, curled up holding my hand.
He says *all my heart all my heart all my heart.*

SPAIN

There is an America here, if you just look for it.
And once there is an America, the rest follows naturally.
They may say that the flowers on our side of the border
Are the same as those six feet to the south, but we know better.
A lot can change in six feet; they know that well enough.

This vehicle contains a safe to which the crew has no access.
Armoured cars move from business to business
taking the money and transporting it elsewhere.
Money as threat, money as identity, identity as threat.
(This country contains a safe to which the crew has no access…)

Their language, which for the time being is our language too,
is full of flourishes, lacks our northern simplicity.
The bigger country was built on forgetting, but forgetting
like you forget in a family, where every detail survives.
There's something to be said for a *pact of oblivion*.

Is there anything to be said for shouting *Long live death*?
Passersby were amazed by the unusual quantities of blood.
The blood flowed right up to the border and then halted,
lapped at the checkpoints and refused to travel any further.
This was unfair, of course: everyone should be allowed blood.

They demanded blood, and were told they already had it.
They demanded x, and were told that the country had no x.
We opened the safe to which we had no access.
Across their country, looking out to sea they notice
the ships that took our troubles away, coming home still heavy.

did i ever say this would be fun
i also said it wouldn't hurt

TO BE CONTINUED

I said the future was built to be ruined:
all rows and colonnades;
architecture of a great sick soul.
Carpet-baggers! Badlings! Scalawags!
Come build in the empty house of the state.
Rich pickings, there is space to occupy,
space to spare, unblemished virgin footage;
leftover voices maybe bubble in the corners.
The self-documented owners of the structure,
wretched in attics and cellars, desperate
for all to be made what it once was
(it never was what it once was, was it?).
The insurgents, fans of a lost
unworkable peasant Communism,
the ones who shouted *Judas!*
when the Soviet Union went electric.
Don't you feel that the structure,
the empire the size of a house,
the house desperate to be an empire,
was all put together very fast?
This machine cannot serve you at the moment.
The house has monetised by-standing;
the crowd never disperses;
the empire makes us sit astounded
in front of the television.
My money doesn't understand me.
I apologise to everyone I ran over in my car.
Thank you for watching this video.
Your reward is 1000 food.

III

OF SHAPES TRANSFORMDE TO BODIES STRAUNGE

An alchemist has to invent
a way out of his own body,
this louche crystal of death.
So, slam your finger hard
in a door. Release a flap
of skin. Breathe oblique on
it. What would the cold air
feel like on your insides?
And now you know what my
schooldays were like.

No one says poetry is truth
twenty-four times a second:
more like a half-made moon
and a sky full of broken glass.
How to draw the line between
that small-souled schoolboy
and the academic having a wank
in the ten minutes before
teaching, in search of mercury?

A splinter in my ring finger.
Black mice. Radiant grape.
I am so heavy the world
always tries to get inside me.
It's anorexia nervōsa, not nervosā.
Not so much what we do in
the shadows, as what the
shadows do in us. The walls ...
my laboratory well-hung
with simples: a dried-out
kohl-eyed kingfisher, a
parasitic moon of mistletoe.

The God of whom I speak is dead.
I did my makeup in a disco ball.
I looked at the whole magnificent
creation of the Lord, and asked,
sadly, 'Is it cake?' Surgeons
operated on him and removed
a living tree from his heart.

PRINCESS

it started when she was a little girl
with her parents fighting
gruff king priam   stiff queen hecuba
all her prophecies phrased as questions

daddy
do you and mummy
hate each other

no no dear calm down
what an imagination she has

the novel of these years could be called
what kassandra knew

and then a little older
for the only time in her life
everyone looked at her
her father   her brother   the god apollo

when she tried to explain
the parallel bruises
hip marks
across her thighs

absent king priam   icy queen hecuba

now think very carefully
these are serious accusations
are you sure   you might be mistaken
gods and parents aren't like that

through the years of being ignored
an embarrassment even after the war

here she stands on stage
alone in a wedding dress
married to her next rapist
screaming the future
suspending time
the nothingness of war

dead king priam   hollow queen hecuba

darling
get off the table
go to your room

sorry about that
she's usually very shy

There was a chuckling spout by the roadside,
a half-hearted run-off to stop the field from clogging.
I thought the landowner had fitted a gargoyle at the end,
the water coming always through his lips. What whimsy!
Water in constant, bright conversation!
I leant my head to it and heard its omens.

A smile of amused curiosity, and those sharp sharp teeth.

Death to the slogan! That morning, my tree had been on fire
with goldfinches, and there was just time to walk
to the church before breakfast. So, past the gargoyle,
so-called, down the overgrown runnel-street,
with finickity hooves clicking on tarmac in the distance.

Then I thought I heard goatbells, clonk-clock coming closer.
The runnel-street, sodden, narrower than I remembered,
narrower than I wanted, didn't seem to go anywhere.
The church. Brambles. My safe word is 'ouch'.
There was a dead magpie lying x-ed by the lychgate.

The churchyard was ruins and tumbled stones;
the light in the empty church was filled with terror.
Door shut close behind me, and I waited while the hooves
and bells went past, finished hunting. Sanctuary,
a rather outmoded notion, yet here and visible:
all you can do is cover your eyes and kneel.

Even if I lived here, this would not be my country.

A coda, because all stories need to end,
and I am here to tell it, so you already know how it ended.
On the way home, the noise of hunting gone,
the goatbells gone, even the winking gargoyle gone.
And in my heart, that never-dying surfeit of water.

A SHORT STORY

He is not cheap, but trust me he has found
the cheapest and hottest hotel room in New Orleans.
The A/C itself is gasping, somehow offended,
and the mosquito net won't hold the little fuckers
back for much longer than tonight at best.
We are here for a conference (*the* conference)
on Peripatetic philosophers, his babies,
and he is to give one of the major papers.
He has said this phrase, 'one of the major papers',
so often that it is no longer comfortable.
It is too hot to wear pyjamas. I lie on top
of the covers, sweating in knickers;
he—I can't believe this—is wearing pyjamas,
a thin pair, buttoned right the way up.
We are almost asleep, a ghost is screaming
in the air-conditioning unit, the night is on us.
And then, through the wall—a cliché of hotels—
the thudding of a bedhead, and voices.
Say my name, comes a man's voice, *say my name*,
and then a pause filled with a woman gasping,
regularly, fulfilled, gasping in happiness or pleasure,
and then the man's voice, *say my name, say my name*.
The tenured professor clears his throat. *Do you think …*
Do you think I should tell him how he sounds,
like a riddle out of the Exeter Book?
I smile, and perhaps he hears my smile.
We lie there until the prime mover stops;
the man has heard his name, and other vocables.
It is still too hot and cheap in this hotel room,
each of us in our own little pool of space,
sweating gently, thinking gently, about to sleep.

I am nearly away, out of the world for one night at least;
his hand reaches through the gap between us.
He touches my thigh and says my name, and I say *yes?*
though I don't know the spin to put on the word.
Darling, could you run to the ice machine?
I did not think that was what he was going to say.
I grunt out of bed, stand swaying in the heat,
shrug on an off-white, ragged dressing gown.
The ice machine is down the corridor,
the corridor is cooler than the room
and the ice machine is calving as I get there.
I open the lid, fill the bucket, stand in the reflected cool.
I turn back after a minute, then hesitate a minute more.
An arrow shows the way back to the room.
Another arrow points out of the world of forms.
What would the Peripatetics do? I smile,
and only I hear my smile. I keep on walking.

FÉLIX FAURE, MAN AND BOAT

Il voulait être César, il ne fut que Pompée

This year, 16 February (same procedure as every year, James),
I acknowledge the death of the President of France,
Félix Faure, in the year eighteen ninety-nine,
of a stiff apoplexy, while receiving oral gratification
from his mistress Marguerite Steinheil.

An appropriate and alternative festival:
orgasm | death, so close to Valentine's Day.
A few years after Faure's death, in nineteen
oh-eight, *President Félix Faure*, a French *quatre-mâts*,
was wrecked off the coast of New Zealand.

Faure sent out lifeboats and made it to land.
No one had died; the island was not a desert.
There was a hut, some short-lived provisions.
Soon they killed albatrosses ('far from tasty')
and after the albatrosses, the penguins.

The birds were quickly traumatised:
after four weeks they shunned *les nouveaux Robinsons*.
I doubt they thought about presidential fellatio
as they hid in the stunted trees
to avoid makeshift spears and nets.

Marguerite Steinheil survived, flourished.
Faure's convulsed hands had tangled in her hair
at *le moment suprême*. At the time of the shipwreck
she was under arrest, accused of killing
her mother and her husband. She got off.

The birds learnt to mistrust mankind.
The sailors survived, were rescued.
Steinheil seduced King Sisowath of Cambodia,
and retired to England, and died in Hove.
Faure remained dead, and ridiculous.

So she died, they all died, man and boat,
and nobody talks about any of this now.
Even I am sorry to speak of such things:
I wear the English cloak of apology.
The English cloak, with a knife beneath the cloak.

BOTTOM'S DREAM

to make it the more gracious, I shall sing it at her death

I remember I carried my only son to bed,
all this is still solid. Just while I fall to sleep,
he said, sit with me just while I fall to sleep.
Just three minutes, just two minutes...
And he was under in thirty seconds,
the yawn still in his mouth, under his tongue.
I left the nightlight plugged in at the wall,
and I was tired and went to bed myself,
next to a warm wife, who sighed in the chaff.

I thought I awoke to a hand, almost marble-smooth,
a voice speaking words I had never known,
a hand that reached up to touch my chest
and a soft generous mouth at my crotch.
After brief confusion I confirmed all this was exact,
but this was not something my wife would do,
so the first question was that of the protagonists:
given this unfaithful staging, this flexible set,
who was the owl, and who the pussycat?

I thought my eyes open, and I still could not see.
I saw in flashes, not enough for one who would try
to describe experience at the moment of living it.
Do you need the scenery? The half-light, the dark
room where I could only see colours darkly;
the head with its skin smoothed to a generic pale;
the straining glans, darker than it should be,
as it bobbed in and out of sight. Did you need all that?
Do you need the pictures of this broken night?

It was an honest dream: in my mind I was
with someone I did not have to lie to.
Perfectly honest, although she was imaginary,
unformed, non-existent, and not my wife.
(Is that an elephant in the room
or are you just pleased to see me?)
I cannot explain, though it always comes back to words,
words and their pleasure building to a head.
Fuck, I said gently, *fuck* (suck on *that*, J.L. Austin!).

Was this one of those times where you take your own life,
take your own life and make it the basis for
the universe? I pressed against her so as to die;
she pressed against me, to bring me back to life.
Or so I hoped, but sudden music in the dream—
the music stuck on repeat in the other room—
belied it, belied and belied and belies it:
Gonna take my Johnny to the graveyard
and I'm damned if I'm bringing him back...

Only this, the music and her face, which I could not see,
but I remember, her skull face at orgasm,
when all energy drained to the contact zones.
Did I understand what I was now?
This was the real world of discrepancy,
and not the idea of the world. I was not-fucking
my not-wife, and the only person I grew closer to
was Death. She radiates silence, like the owl.
Death on a pale horse, gentlemen. Let's roll.

The dream was fading as the end drew near.
The oral form of love is the end of democracy.
It is feudalism, the rich choking the poor.
It is a photograph at the end of photographic time,

the statue with her high torch, and that verdigrised,
smoke-stained plaque that only reads GIVE ME.
And now, the swimmers into cleanness leaping.
I woke up ashamed, in hoarse and messy sheets.
And these, these words, what did they taste like?

THE IDYLL REPLACED BY AN UNJUSTIFIABLE MELANCHOLY

Before us we have a picture & I would like you to come
to it with me. It is a small thing & shouldn't take long.
I don't promise knowledge, or that it will be painless.
The picture is a Soviet landscape large as a portfolio.
It is a bright landscape & maybe I would maybe say happy.
I've only seen it on a postcard which I sent to you blank.
The question of dimensions has been raised & passed over.
I am unaware what it represents, it is a field & a tree
but the title is given different in Russian & English,
perhaps both Russian & English are needed here.
The English title says it is the picture of a tree.
The Russian title says it is the picture of a field.
It is say the picture of a single upright stroke in white oil
surrounded by dormant & yielding green & yellow oils,
& it is say the picture of the field returning on itself
with a lonely rowan-tree stiff in the background.
I understand it all ways; language is not my friend
& only covers a world that is not of itself anything.
Tansy and mountain ash are in the picture, & my understanding
is not in the picture & the picture is not my friend.
I do not know the names for what any of this is.
When I come to ask what you think, there is no answer.
& you have not been here for too long.

lovers lonely in the dark
when practice turns to theory
here: once an exclamation mark
now a mournful query

IV

DEAD DEER

Great stuffed wineskin of a deer, dead deer, lying up against the fall,
next the lost punt pole and the abandoned tyre, tyre bleached in the sun,
water running over the weir, over arched-back head and body, the body swollen
little more each day, the eyes and bent legs oddly untouched, the deer still,
perfect, still perfect. I pray to this idol, little god of defeat, father of our failures,
overseer of the torn and defeated, shattered vase, vestigial tail;
I stand there daily to look at it, the whittering of pigeons under the bridge,
the same pigeons, children, great-grandchildren of the birds there
when I threw an engagement ring off the bridge eighteen years ago,
pigeons who exploded in an applause of wings and sour sheet metal
against the grainy sky of the five a.m. sleepless walk, walk whose only purpose
was the deliberate loss of the ring, and now, useless, I am married to her:
find someone you like to look at who doesn't hate you, they said. Enough.
The deer has been there four or five days now, hardly Shakespeare,
hardly enough to build a religion on; heron ignores it, mallards skim by.
I walked out this morning, to go to town, to pass the weir, to see the silenced
muntjac, vast as a dog, unnatural, bloated, silent, placid, unlikely seed:
the cat stood at the top of the stairs, and as I left I stroked him
and *love* he said *you think I need your love?* The cat stood at the top of the stairs
as I passed by, sardonic, alone, unopened, unfair, turning his head against me,
when other times, other days, he presses his mouth into my palm,
silences himself, growls within himself, sits on my lap when I try to teach.
Blockade cat, blunt cat against my walking. The river says you are married.
I dreamt for a while that a gigantic fish would swallow the ring, that I would live
to see somewhere in the *faits divers*, the local news, the miraculous story,
the gutted fish and a triumphant Polish fisherman, silent and sardonic
holding the carat and a half between two slabby fingers. It never happened;
my son still dreams of dredging the river, as if time did nothing and the river
flowed too slowly to lose the ring again. The river says again that you are married.
You can argue all you want; house and wife, libraries, shared children,
you are married, the pillow is never alone again, the dead breast is yours alone.
Stuffed, swollen wineskin of a deer, muntjac, dead, pushing up against the weir:
God's kingdom advances through glorious victories, cleverly disguised as disasters.

COLD

It was a smug film, smug on its own evil, fat with it,
the actor-king so smug, the direction, allegedly so cold, so pure,
in fact only smug-drunk on its ambience of slush and nicotine,
springtime and grey city light and all the poor beige suicides,
the camera always moving, side to side, more fear, more broken
people, the surrounders, who indulged their man's brokenness,
the always sense of a wink to the camera, of men complicit in their
acting, their actions. *I want to know nothing*—this is not grief,
this is a teenage boy's, an Italian's fantasy of grief, how to weaponise
grief, grief as the royal road to a woman's body—and we tell the
audience that she is unsatisfied, and she keeps coming back
doesn't she, she's asking for everything that is filmed and shown,
and the great statue, Brando collapsing, Brando shouting,
the reason for all this, the centrepiece, his grunting
the audible sign of a *great actor*, just how close can you approach
a full contempt for the audience and still pivot on their love,
Brando grunting and dangerous even through the screen. One moment
in this vast smug film, black stain on the negative, when
I tell you I felt as pure a cold as any art has ever made me feel,
when Jeanne shouts across the metro station, a train passing,
to her useless and aggressive boyfriend, screams in a fury she
deserves *je suis fatigué de me faire violer* | *I am tired of being raped*
and the train passes and she has her fury out in the world
and that clever-clever camera switches to show how she is seeing
and there is no one standing or listening on the other platform.

And I saw this film in the cold cinema, the Spartak cinema,
the unheated former Lutheran church on Kirochnaya Street,
in 2001, before it was destroyed in an insurance fire,
in spring, almost spring, I was unhappy, not that unhappy, in love.
The film a scratched print, the sound horrid, the underpaid

abused *lektor* read out the script in a dry Russian monotone,
and the film was so cold, the church so cold, the camera eye so too …
I did not deserve to feel so cold, but what saved me was the world
existing outside the film, the cinema, the church, the abyss,
that voyeur, always ready with a few home truths, and to know that
yes, there was always standing and listening and watching,
and you can see the world without judgement and knowledge, it is not
all grey and tired, even in the grey-tired, grey-skinned city.
I came out into the grey evening, and forced myself to see life,
and that evening the bridges opened like a great stone bible,
and the river, the frozen river, the river, tore pages from itself.

ANEKDOT

Another city poem, another anecdote.
St Petersburg. The band we saw that evening
Was *Полтора Кило Отличного Пюре,** which translates as
A Kilo and a Half of Excellent Mashed Potatoes.
Jeez, lighten up; it was the millennium, Jesus.

Sample lyrics: 'I walk through my
native microregion | hacking at
lapdogs with a large axe.' Where are they now,
would be a fair question. Even Russia
can't sustain all types of cynicism forever.

A basement red-brick, with a crammed bar—
a little bit ayurvedic café, a little bit
cult HQ—and while Jeremy went to *blue*
with the dickstickers, which translates as
whatever the hell you want it to mean,

I drank there with you, and it was almost erotic.
Although mostly it was pornographic:
a crammed bar, and no one caring.
When you said *let's get out of here*,
I asked *why* and you shrugged. *Fair point.*

People went through and disappeared
from our lives back then, hostels and beds.
When a few years later I found myself
in your Berlin, I wrote you a long Leonard
Cohen-y email, which I don't think you

---

* The band's name is pronounced *Poltorá Kiló Otlíchnovo Piuré.*

ever answered. Spam folder, perhaps.
Friends of friends sent me rumours
but even those petered out, bored:
did you get hoovered | god | a wife | true
communism on earth. Delete as inappropriate.

I moved on. Yeah, I'm totally all over
all this. This is my life, nor am I out of it:
I'm a shark, sleek and total, dead-eyed.
Where am I now, is always the only question.
Jeez, it was the millennium. Lighten up. Jeez-o.

NEW YEAR POEM

Nobody knows anything. Nobody knows anything:
that's the slogan. Let *Nobody knows anything*
be the whole of the law. The newspapers snigger,
but *nobody knows anything;* prediction headlines
tell us nothing, unless 2025 really will be
as suggested, *the year that incest comes into its own.*
The present, that brief pool of certainty,
is choppy and unwelcoming, nothing but lies
and judgement, passed on and ignored by liars.
As so often, the only hope is the verifiable past.
Am I happy about this? Am I happy? Am I balls.
But when you name something you make it visible,
and the soft present is filled with too many names.
The old year folds into the new year's arms.
Someone else's sentence as a springboard:
The conversation ran first on different types of tobacco
and then, entirely naturally, moved onto women...
So, Blue Gauloises. And her name was Ira,
and the *dies Irae* lasted a couple of weeks if that,
and nothing memorable happened during.
Apart from this: we went to visit a friend of hers,
in a village that did not yet exist, a tower block
in the middle of fields, the making-visible
of that old slogan *Coming Soon: Picturesque Ruins.*
A place that did not yet have its own genius.
I can't remember what we did, only the husk
of an outing to the uninhabited husk of a society:
views of long fields inviolate of thought
end in horizon, a rising line of trees.
Erratic tower block that seemed to proclaim
henceforth we will live in a world without memory.

This is the aim of all usurpers: to make us forget
that they have only just arrived.
You see this memory is the same as what
I was fleeing: the present squashed into the past,
and the future a crushed version of the present.
Ira's father was the captain of an icebreaker:
one other thing I remember. The ship that passes
through the ice that closes up again behind it.
The eternal present, choppy and unwelcoming.
Ira's father. #hertoo. Everything can be weaponised,
even love. We are all owned and we all own others.
Men resemble their times more than their fathers,
and that was another new year. The new year, always
born from its old body like a scorpion moults,
through the the mouth, shit of its own mouth.
We find ways both concrete and absolute to be ruined.

TWO PUBLIC SCHOOLBOYS, WALKING OVER SKELETONS

When the first snows came we changed our walk to work
—for certain definitions of work, for certain definitions of walking—
we skiddered the mile downhill to the grey-block Philology building
with its lagged-pipe smell and mildly lecherous faculty.

Moscow was savage that winter: they devalued the currency,
but that didn't make us, dollar supported, any the richer
(it's no use having money if the shops sell only vodka and cheese)
and we lost weight and walked rather than spend 20 roubles bussing it.

The snows were thick and sudden and the city changed with them,
became more purposeful, sadder, more of itself, stank less,
and somehow yes, it's what snow does, more innocent.
Snow is a useful stand-in for actual innocence.

So we slid on packed snow and ice for months from November
and taught our classes and explained grammar via Dylan lyrics
to resentful students who were gulpingly avid to learn
but also upset they had to learn from us.

There were plus points, like when I was left at home for an evening,
and the whole filthy flat was mine for a few hours,
so I read a little while, then put on the Ella Fitzgerald cassette,
and heard 'Love for Sale' as snow fell against the orange streetlights.

But interactions with real people, discussions, humanity…
they all went on in their bearable, slightly angry fashion:
the snow covering things up till you forgot about them,
grew angry again, learnt more, waited for more snow.

When the thaw kicked in, maybe round April, a month before their exams,
we carried on walking by what we still called the new route.
One day in the slush something cracked under my feet:
I looked down on a stray dog's white ribcage, skull grin, some hair.

Two public schoolboys, walking over skeletons.
More and more corpses came to light as the snows receded.
We were going to leave the country, so what could we do?
What we did was just that: leave and remember so little.

SHE TOLD ME THIS STORY ...

She told me this story: in a different flat
one late spring day, a swift fell into her bedroom.
It lay still and scared, breathing fast and still.

Telling the story, a slave's inspiration, she knelt
to the floor, her wrists pinioned behind her back
to show how the swift had fallen.

It progressed, how she had scooped the bird
into her resolute hands and held it unresisting
to the window, how it had been thrown out

and failed to fly, how it had fallen down the well
between the flats, and landed neatly,
and lain waiting for the local cat.

How she had run downstairs, knocked on every door
until an old Chinese woman had let her climb
through a ground floor window onto the tiles

(the Chinese woman was never seen again,
had maybe never existed), how she had carried
the bird, unspilled, upstairs in her hands.

And this second time, how she had held the swift
further out, waited for it to unship its wings, how it had
scrabblingly launched itself to a world it understood.

(The next time she gave me this story,
she was with her then boyfriend,
and he was telling her not to help.)

with you an opera any opera
where I can sit beside you in the dark
to watch other people die

Cuntstruck, and seeking no human company, I ended up among the classical statues, that shorthand for boredom in any museum. But there, musing on you, with you in my head, I stayed rapt looking for ten minutes at a perfect small statue of Venus. The sculptor a keen improviser: a blemish in the marble made her right nipple. I stared beyond the bounds of propriety or even artistic need. Pervert Pygmalion, as I try to force my memory of your living flesh to this marble: almost, by the strength of my imagination, to bring you here to my side. You must make sure your life stays exactly the same.

PORTRAIT WITH HINDSIGHT

Two anonymous people—
clinging on, shipwreck-tight—
sway and hug, head on shoulder,
in a dark kitchen, years ago.
Would I really *give my life*
for those too few weeks again,
as I said in one letter?
Those letters, polite as passports …
though we took nude Polaroids,
so we'd always have bookmarks.
(No chance of blackmail after
a decade of beer and meat
made me clearly someone else;
still, when you sent mine back, cut
to neat squares, anxiety
vanished overnight, like a circus.)
But why are you back here, now?
If this year has taught me
anything at all, it's this:
if I'm close enough to know
your perfume, I am in danger.
Maybe you are curious:
I think of ghosts as curious.
You're back in scents and glimpses,
the migraine-pulse of memory.
I notice you in doorways
where you never stood. I went out
with my wife and you were there,
at the restaurant table,
last in the black procession—
waiter, sommelier, you—

the same amused, ballsy smile:
I came to see what she looks like.
Your fist shook, half-serious:
He was mine! A fly buzzed
in the distanced dining room.
The truest test of love, to love
independently of space—
I was never here with you.
You stand at every corner.
I wrote that in a letter, too.
Our irreversible life …
I'm overwhelmed with the past:
I'd swear I heard you singing
a few days back, a cool summer
evening, half-time moon.
No, you can't fuck Farida
if you won't pay Farouk …
I am nothing but memory;
you are nothing but memories:
life we ruin as we live it.
Hold on to this, when all else goes:
the cold kitchen at dusk,
the garden out there, unseen,
unseeing, all of it suspended,
two anonymous people—
shipwreck-tight, head on shoulder—
in a dark kitchen, years ago.

1.

I swallow a pill filled with black television static. In my situation notebook, before the scholarly exercise breaks down into vague sketched parallel lines, there is a comment: 'Marvellous nightmares!' The handwriting is not mine.

My daughter eats cherries like something out of *La Bohème*. Another speckled handkerchief drops to the floor. She gives a vast, contented, operatic sigh, then reaches her determined fat-knuckled hand to the bowl again.

At the beginning of all this, I went for illicit dawn bike rides down empty B-roads. I crossed the motorway bridge with no traffic underneath me; stopped once dead at a vast buck hare, calm in the middle of the tarmac.

Of course, an anagram of the whole Bible would also be the whole Bible.

I have recently discovered Berlioz's *Les nuits d'été*. As with all new art, I wait for someone to tell me that my taste is faulty; that I cannot, must not, am simply forbidden from enjoying them.

I want to say something here about my father.

2.

I have to learn new techniques to think about my family. I cannot, must not live always along the same metaled ways. I must stop e.g. thinking of my parents as boring, start thinking of them as cruel.

I find my daughter with a recognizable face—my own face, when I am caught in some avoidable naughtiness. With my little finger I remove a cheerfully disarticulated woodlouse from her mouth. The thorax bitten into three crunchy chunks.

I cannot rely on my own powers of criticism. Not here, not in 'real' life. What I need is extra: a loose word or an unguarded comment will do, in default of a full deathbed confession.

The old riddle talks about cherries. You begin with a handful of flesh, and end with a few scattered jack-bones.

Evenings when we didn't play backgammon, we would play Scrabble. I would always lose. The draughty table, the concentrated silence. The avant-jazz of a butterfly trapped in the paper lampshade above us.

Or else this: the broad empty road underneath me; too early for birdsong. Two sinister motionless herons. A light moving in the sky.

3.

Nothing ever as empty as those darktime streets. Even the golden light in the window, the *sotto voce* hum of some recorded opera ... even this is not enough. You start to believe in the patchy folk history of this area: weird beasts in the fields, the one-eyed dog.

For some people, his knowledge and sympathy is immense. Others are accepted on sufferance, if at all. I know that the open scars in my knowledge are things he has agreed to ignore; the mask slips occasionally. You should suffer fools joyously.

We're not getting out of this alive. Fortune favours the grave. #NoLivesMatter

I cannot remember if I was given a knife. Probably not: we pulled apart terrified buds of the hollyhocks with our nimble childish fingers. The colour was never inside them, never the deep cherry-stain we desired. Hollyhocks and honesty both.

We ordered the detritus in such a way as to tell the future. Poor man, beggarman.

Auguries are always unreliable, as unreliable as good taste. The sibyl, with god-aid, speaks with her maddened lips things both blunt and serious. The thousand-year reach of her voice.

4.

For *x* read *y*. Story of my life.

Before all this began, in heat, I walked five miles to the isolated boarding-house. Luck had me meet her on the road, slightly tipsy, freewheeling. 'What, are *you* here!' I have often played that curt sentence in my head, reading and misreading its emphasis.

The morning greets us with a glass of water and a bowl of fridge-cold cherries. Desultory love-talk before the inevitable, clandestine parting.

So many things I have kept from those closest to me, among which a reassessment of who those closest to me really are. Close in terms of affection, or close in terms of likeness?

After one such disaster, a trip to the chemist for Duprisal 30. The motherly pharmacist, a man approaching retirement, takes her by the sleeve and says 'Now, don't do that again, eh?' I had not thought her so obedient.

Another curtailed fatherhood. Duprisal, reprisal … Something along those lines.

5.

Oh, headlong immorality! Oh, driving license!

I gave my truncated Oberon, in a production that I insisted no one come to see. I remember very little. 'Of thy misprision must perforce ensue | Some true love turned, and not a false turned true.'

In the sweated bedroom, the shared flat, there was always a video on in the background. For some weeks it has been *Without a Clue*, or else *Magnolia*, or else *The Matrix*. Writing this, it has taken me some time to remember these titles. Rabbit holes, rabbit holes.

From the roadside. Hare forms in the grass. A slight depression. *Nadie nos ha visto.*

Brother of mine lives now in a village, just too far to reach easily by bike. I am in awe of how he has gathered a family to himself, working with children and animals.

A themed picnic for his daughter's first birthday. Salami, lollipops, cherry pie, sausages, all with neat holes eaten through them.

6.

At the beginning of all this, I was alone and dazed. On the evening after the vote, I ate a bowl of ripe, solid cherries macerated in dark rum and dark sugar. A little expensive vanilla ice-cream. *My* world was alright, for a few minutes.

He flies like Icarus. Alas for his wings!

Slower now than he was, and less present. How much of a person's existence depends on others' noticing them? Old men ought to be spies.

But maybe I have been wrong the whole time? I remember when I was a child, enthralled, waiting for the next gnomic clue, scrap of wisdom. A few words in that calm, slow voice. I built a world on them, a religion. And now, hardy recusant, loyal dunce, I worry the façade is all there is, all there ever was.

I saw him from behind, riding his bicycle up the only hill. I could have overtaken him walking. You cannot see my face.

Neat in a box, with many lids like little television screens. Medicine to walk you from Monday to Sunday.

7.

A handful of pills; a handful of cherries; a handful of pills. Anita eats cherries like Mimi. My son told me a joke, his version of a joke: *Who was the first man to die? God, because he had to die to become God.* I felt nothing except knowledge and terror.

The lights failed halfway round his circuit, and he rode the last seven miles in frightened darkness, hoping for the dawn at every corner. Calmed himself, partially, by remembering crossword clues.

A book on 'the soul of rugby', *Muddied Oafs*. I misread the title as *Murdered Osiris*. Now, *there's* something to tell the old man!

I WRITE YOU A LETTER

over the long course of an afternoon
with the eggshell sky losing its colour
turning from blue to grey-black
all the light leaching from the world
until the world is black
and the letter is full of light

… because it is in kingdoms as it is in gross bodies …

I.

The key difference being between those who are paid weekly,
those who are paid monthly, and those who never pay at all,
preferring (as who would not prefer?) to live within money,
to have this faint negotiable atmosphere surround them,
discreet gold rings, gaudy gold teeth, golden bones, lungs
full of gold.

Where is Death in this picture? Don't make me laugh. Death
is everywhere—the sand is Death, the forever crawl and rush
of water on shells and rocks, animals rolled on animals, broken
into crystals and fragments of an ebbed consciousness. The
coins in my wallet … render Death unto Death, mint new
Death, strike the face of Death.

Every fist of sand with its tiny hermit crab—the largest as
long as my thumbnail—reaching out a small defiant claw.

II.

We stand in the doorway and watch your ghost
and my ghost together, interlaced on the dirty mattress.
Four years of leasehold dust—the poverty in the air,
the bride stripped bare by her investors.

With half-closed melancholy, we watch these earlier
iterations of our love: rapt limbs, hungry mouths.
Lovers should know to bring no gift,
if no suitable gift can be found. No home.

Leave me alone, bloody love, leave me alone;
landlords, abandon me; plague keep to your doors.
I have obeyed the restrictions to their ever-changing letter,
spirit and flesh, ghost and trembling bone.

III.

A message from a distant friend: the sand in these photographs
looks like an actor's rice powder. Did the wind blow your
footsteps back towards Africa?

The street sweepers, grinding machines that rifle through the
sand and dead cockroaches, dampen the dogshit and beer cans.
Fifteen minutes after they are gone, all smells of urine once
again. I love this town, town of stroke victims and volleyball
players, together in the sand, daring a hypnotic and begging
sun.

The sad streets, overshadowed daily by the fifteen-storey
ferry—the city needs this more than ever, this floating indolent
money, that may or may not land here, sporing its largesse, as
it feels. The ship's horn echoes in the squares. Soon it will be
leaving.

It's like I ate the ocean and spat out all the salt.

DWELLING

Coffee, an expresso, the morning's confessional,
and a scrap of cardboard from a listless envelope:
Miss Desire to Mister Desired, a phone number,
all written in her scratchy ungirlish hand.
The card torn from a knock-off perfume box,
all the false expensive gold and brown.
You can tell this is a memory, can't you;
her number gone the way of tickets and bookmarks,
lost and reassembled like everything piecemeal.
If I had the number still I might dial it,
that lost Russian flat, and feign surprise
when someone who was not her answered me
or the call rang out in an empty house.
    I am thinking a lot about something my son said—
you know that 'memory' means 'mirroring enemy'?—
though I don't know where that came from
or why he should have said it now, when it hit hard.
Family reflections …

                        I tried to find it once
one afternoon years ago: I left my wife in the hotel—
not bruised, not twenty-one, reading a suitable book—
and took the metro into the past, the part
of my past closest to Mayakovskaya station.
I thought it would be stamped in my body
and my feet would move without thinking
through the courtyards and the Soviet architecture,
the portals and podyezds.

                        But then: was this it, the flat?
Was it here? Was I ever here? Or here?
I walked through doorways and under arches.
I waited until one set of heavy gates opened

and a bullish black-metalled car came out,
then I nipped through as the gates pulled slowly shut.
Was this it, then? A courtyard I couldn't place,
a fountain that hadn't been there before?
     What was I doing, running after a ghost?
My calm wife back in the hotel, my family, a future,
and me here to dig up the dead and impossible.
Stupid, stupid James.
                                        The water was speaking,
and a woman was speaking to her child
in one of the ground floor flats.
The gates had closed, and for twenty minutes
I thought I might be here forever,
coded into the courtyard, blocked and lost.
Then of course, no melodrama, nothing,
the gates came open to admit a man with shopping bags
and recalled to life I left, to go home.
While I paced distracted, I heard the woman
make a nice distinction to her attentive child:
серебряный, не серебристый! Not silver-plate—silver, silver!

i drag my finger
over your skin and hope
to hear it sing like glass

v

MUSEUM

distracted by yourself you do not notice
until it is much too late
(it has always been much too late)
the alabaster gods surrounding your exhibit
unreadable eroded expressions on their faces

CASSANDRA

I.

I was thinking about Cassandra, who shows and does not tell. Or rather, who tells and does not tell, but that's a weak pun to stick on a victim.
Her loneliness, and then the way she contains, like all prophets, the whole of the future.

Also the past. I was about twelve or thirteen. It was an unexpected present. A starter microscope.
I remember the texture of it, the rough-brushed metal of the body, the chrome smoothness of the eyepiece and the lenses.

Time is, often said, a form of sandpaper. It is only in still-rough scraps that I can recall just how rancid my adolescence was.
During last year's plague I watched a livestream from my school and felt sick the whole time.

And yes, the impossibility of writing about God. Reading the *Comedy* for the first time, discovering that Paradise, even for Dante, is a form of erasure.
The detail and focus of the earlier books replaced by the scouring whiteness of the Lord.

There are some seasons that we have lost, some that have become sharpened beyond endurance.
Summer is now an enemy, and a fly-ridden and seemingly eternal yellow autumn is what takes the place of the lost and desired winter.

In one of my books, the little green Loeb edition of *The Trojan Women*, I keep a jay's feather as a bookmark.

I like to read parallel texts, all the unknown language screaming past on the verso, pages turned twice as fast.

Me? Just sitting here, one side of the Greek, that beautiful alien alphabet, a page-world of slant words and harsh breathing.
... δέκα γὰρ ἐκπλήσας ἔτη | πρὸς τοῖσιν ἐνθάδ᾽, ἵξεται μόνος πάτραν ... *Another ten years on top of the war, and then a lonely journey to his lone homeland, only to find more cares.*

The dark band on the feather fills the space gap between the blue-white striations towards the vane and the fade to grey at the quill. Feather the story of a sparrow's flight.
Sure, I'd been lonely, but never lonely enough to find myself in the prefects' room completely aware of what was going to happen.

Water. Yellow leaves by the window. He offered me water afterwards, to help with the bitterness in my mouth. It was he gave me the microscope. I thought that was kindness.
I'm open to the past now, been helped to talk about it. Pleased to hear some people say it doesn't exist, that all's only present. That's a mercy.

But the dance of the year, year after year unceasing. Exhaustion. *Café Müller*, with our eyes closed rushing across the stage in blocked surrender.
It's touch that keeps the dance together. Abnormal sensitivity to touching and being touched. I sleep outside the marriage bed.

Very male, my kind of failure. Repeated circling of the same words that I can't say, actions I can't carry out. A life relocated offline.
And the years between twelve and seventeen, all that time. Minefields of discovery against a background of general unhappiness.

Sorry, but I can't get over it: we're meant to think Paradise is a place of absence? Of removal? I would like to speak of what I see, if I ever go there.

If I ever go anywhere. This is corona-time, the long dark days as the year drains out. We are made unsafe by the state. *Created sick, commanded to be sound*: who said that?

The answer grevilling away at the edge of my mind. I remember liking that poem, when I was young and in Russia, before all of this and after all of that.
I used to have it by heart, even: ... *Nature herself doth her own self deflower |*
To hate those errors she herself doth give ...

Yet when each of us in his own heart looks | He finds the God there, far unlike
his books. (I do not know much about gods, but I think my god must be a wizened, petty god.)
And the whole time Cassandra stands there, screaming what will happen, screaming until she's hoarse, until her throat bleeds. She never breaks.

She should be played by a teenager, sitting at the family table, aware of the adult life above her she cannot pierce or enter.
Vomiting herself light as a feather, her wristbones the rachis and calamus of a feather, she is all voice, turned on tuned in tuned out turned out.

I first knew about her in childhood. She seemed scared and somehow terrifying. Like if there was a ghost and you would say *There's a ghost* and they would say *No there isn't*.
Coming home from school alone, spending the holidays alone, enjoying the loneliness.

The futon where I slept for five years of holiday, folding and unfolding it morning and evening. I can still feel that wicked cotton.
And the mattresses in Russia, the threadbare student dorm. The yellow corona of grease at the head end, the yellow corona of old urine at waist level. Sheets halfway to nets.

Winter a time for the dead. The dead moan to the living *why must you always haunt us?* No one cares for this place, with its undistinguished churches. Winter now itself dead.

Sorry again, I got unstuck there for a moment. Who cares about the past, when we have the future repeating ahead of us?

II.

Well, the microscope. I remember sand, and blood, and small crustacea on the preprepared slides. I remember whole worlds of sand, the surprising order of blood.

We're world-taught about the symmetry of small things at the moment. How regularity is easier in the viral world between life and death.

And I need no microscope to see the chaos forming where we live. The butterfly's wings expand beyond their limits: come stroll down Cyclone Alley!

(Live Professor Lazarus speaks of a *wicked problem*. Uncertainties and circularities that defy resolution.)

I lived through the coldest winter in Moscow's history, and would do so again. Veins burst in my nose. Piss froze on its way to the snow.

I remember we went to the reopened church, full of people wanting human warmth and candles. Friendship and secondarily God. The steps frozen glib.

On the thick lake ice our feet sang. When touched, it shaved layers of your skin so gently that blood was the first warning. I note all of this because it will not happen again.

The lakes will not freeze again. The churches will remain open; their congregations will dwindle. History lays down a marker.

But all this is in the future. Look now at the sad boy, his eye to the ocular lens, the weak torch bulb unearthly through the stain of a butterfly's wing.

Later, the knock at the door, the letters from home, the stupid camaraderie,

the false bonhomie, the first few times—setup, punchline—he drinks to
forget.

Undaunted by what appears to be success, he moves in his head from
disaster to disaster. A fall from the stars.
Fallen so far that the stars mean nothing to him, neither the decaying
planet. Here, here, the coarse focus, the fine focus, the hooklets on the
jay's feather, here!

III.

Bare-headed, face to the ground, he finds things that other people laugh
at him for finding. That feather, yes, and feather-eaten leaves. Eggshells,
stones, sometimes money.
It's good practice, my therapist says, for *the unhappy Present to recite the Past
like a poetry lesson*. Did I say therapist?

Parsing the past, but there remains some insoluble core from which no
sample can be taken. All text is in places corrupt.
Breathe it in, try to breathe it out, the whole plaguey world. You are not
Caesar just by breathing Caesar's air. (Render this, cocksucker!)

The ritualised exchange of glances and catcalls at school, as chilling in its
way as any expression of courtly love. Know your place, peon. Peon, you
are no Beatrice.
So much of what we call tradition is sixty years old at best. How far can we
look outside the present? Not far enough to save ourselves.

Memories, so the song goes, don't leave like people do. In fact, Cassandra has
often curled up alone, the sharp-clawed past drawing blood from the inside.
Memory also means *fame*. So much celebrity, she calls out, so much pop-
star adulation, all shrinking to this: the red bathtub, the sheet become a
shroud.

Her gift, *ihr Gift*, came somehow from Apollo. She refused to marry him, and he punished her. When she says *no* people will hear *yes*.
She remembers yellow leaves by the window. The yellow glow of his armour. His face a yellow blur above her. Prophecy comes when you're fucked in the mouth.

Again and again, rachis and calamus, retching and wretched. For some months afterwards she lost her sense of touch. Everything felt like black ice.
Siblings, the gods are; a mafia family you don't want to upset. Is Cassandra then *made* by the gods? What is this constant unheeded speech, her *omertà*?

A god, one god, many gods. Crowding round her in her sleep, inside her head. *You are a story teller*, they say. Gods are smaller than we imagine.
Their idea of mercy is to turn you into stars, birds, trees, flowers, spiders, any of the jigsaw that makes up what they believe the renewing world.

Cassandra would have liked to be an iris. A flower that fills and then breaks the cup of itself. Cassandra would like to have been noticed.
Today the tombs are corrupt, their heroes in museums. There is no one who will cut even a dog's throat to make them an offering.

Her mouth opens, and there is radio static in her listeners' ears. She speaks with absolute teenage clarity, and they see a yellow blur. Don't look straight at the sun.
Abruptly, they allow her to leave the stage. Her last words are not to tell us that death shall have no victory, but that she shall come to death victorious.

Before this, she talks of the boy. *To be blunt, he will go through Hell alive, and through the salt water, and his troubles will not end at his front door.*
I heard this the first time I read it, just as I hear it now in these untested times. Her voice spoke to me; I thought myself the first to believe her.

Did she speak out loud? I doubt it. I had other voices in my head at that time. But even in this knock-kneed translation of a hobbled play, I met her.

This path peters out. I'll leave for now my past here. Go away, you nauseating adolescent.

Hide in your work, your books, the microscope that was your suckled reward. It is not I hope possible to die of loneliness in a crowd.

I dream of ice shelves thick as skyscrapers, calving worried icebergs so wide you could barely range a missile across them.

IV.

I see it, what you once called the forest. I see the fertile soil turned to breckland, the sand too loose to hold roots. The fen blow, the dust tornadoes.

I see God's fingerprints all over this. His helplessness, apologies. His promise that is also a threat. The steering wheel pulled hard one way, then the other.

I see the end of family life, the victory of the self, people moving along the lines of self like pillbugs. Unable to touch, curling to themselves when touched.

I see our leaders; I see the passenger pigeon, the dodo, the labrador duck, the cuban macaw, the eskimo curlew, the spectacled cormorant, the great auk.

I see them all, both high and low, the great rulers and the ruined teenage boy. Unmoored from his life, clamped to any form of love that offers itself.

I see the razed beds. The frivolous gardens lost to necessary and insufficient use. Envious show dissolves to hardscrabble; subsistence on friable dirt.

I see the victories of language, language accepting two battles, language both denatured and specific, the only permissible language the press-release and the in-crowd slang.

I see this happening now.

I see the self once again, the desire for a client state, the reflex desire for an absolute and unmasked freedom. Intention will not matter, and all behaviour will be bad behaviour.
I see an odd summer, with never no dark clouds gathering. I see the rain and think It can't rain like this forever. *I see the parched and sodden grass.*

She is curled on her mattress. That prophesying, unwilling and uncontrolled. The muttered future at her lips. She picks eternally at her nails; draws blood.
An orderly ups the dosage. A few words of what Cassandra says are distinguishable; none of them makes any coherent sense.

V.

Any relationship with another human being, even if lasting and meaningful, especially if failed and transitory, must take place within Nature, and must be subject to her laws.
Those laws. The Spanish definition of man as a rule-breaking animal. The bright wild rose opens her sepals, here, in late December.

It's good Cassandra never saw this coming, that she was still able to believe that revenge has a use, that the art of winning had been *to die off first.*
It's the gods I feel sorry for myself. Olympus shrunken to a few small half-sacred groves and stones. Your altars crumble. Your temples the backgrounds to selfies.

The first day of a new year, shirtsleeves and open collar, I take a walk with my family. All blossomed. The rose blushes yellow beyond the frosted glass.
What you aim for by walking is to forget your discontent. Temporary stasis *en route.* Even though memory assembles worlds of wretchedness.

The sun was dressed in winter haze this morning, but now the sky is total unforgiving blue, the kind of blue I should like to overcome me.
I look up into the sun. Shield your eyes. A herring gull twists above, a knife

against the light, and disappears.

Through how many years shall this day travel? My throat feels tight; there is no time in the room. Annushka has already spilled the oil.

The face in the mirror has said something upsetting. My vanity the vanity of a younger man, still brave enough to look into the glass without knowing what he'll see.

So many questions remain unanswered, but I know I would rather make up an answer than live without one. *Hachi garsinan.*

And evening comes, as evening always comes, with all the pencil shades of the winter sky.

VI.

Gone beyond! Gone beyond! Gone far beyond! Gone to the far shore! Awakened! The rough gate opens.

And all beyond is briars and tangles. Progress, if there is progress, is desperate. First one leg sticks, and then the other is hooked still.

Nostalgia, n. the pain of returning home. *Nostos, n.* a homecoming, the conclusion of a literary work. Nostalgia covers everything, but it was sad, super sad.

And are we back to the enemy summer? Sun-dead tomatoes. You say tomato, I say tornado. There are furies at the bottom of my garden.

We don't remember this. We remember the odd May snow. We remember the exciting sky, bruised and groaning green. We remember lightning.

A voice from the east, a voice from the west, a voice from the four winds, a voice against Jerusalem and the temple, a voice against bridegrooms and brides, a voice against the whole people.

But we are deluding ourselves (and there's nothing new about that).
Prophecy demands voices, but there will be no voices.
We imagine an uninhabited world, but one we can see. The plains free for
us to walk on. No gods to bend our ears. We are imaging the past.

A cormorant flew above our heads as we returned home. The Jurassic line
unbroken and yet about to break. I have seen them rejoicing their wings
in the treetops.
I spent too much time drawing autumn leaves last year. While I was mad,
while I was permitted to be mad.

Now I am permitted to be sane, and here I am, sane as anything. A high
temperature and a new continuous cough. I never had much of a sense
of taste.
Why are you walking with me through all this? I never asked you to come.
So many things happened to me unwilled.

Why are you walking with me through all this? I never asked you to come.
So many things happened to me unwilled.
I have spent years thinking about a few instants of touch.

We should not forget about time, though we are asked to on so many
occasions. They would like us to live in timeless panic.
τὸ τῆς ἀνάγκης δεινόν: ἄρτι κἀπ᾽ ἐμοῦ | βέβηκ᾽ ἀποσπασθεῖσα Κασάνδρα
βίᾳ. *Needs must; a sublime force. Cassandra has been taken away from me, just
now, just like that.*

Seemingly eternal yellow autumn came to an end of course. The barometer
swings. All the weather! At once!
I don't think I'm particularly complex, but I know I'm unreliable. It is an
achievement to attain and believe such niceties.

... now ruined and on fire, and I a mother bird screaming over her
children will begin my song ... | ... shore echoes to our cries,

and as a bird bewails its young so we bewail our husbands ...
... now ruined and on fire ... Ilium is burning: let us lament aloud.

He won't ever let up, will he, God? He comes back and back again, a voice
   fiercely loyal to its one great octave.
Is it normal to feel scared, coming home? The childish moment of coming
   home? I feel sober | hungover | terrified.

This irreversible life. What I like best about the old days is that they're over.
Cassandra saw something else: a woman dressed in black furs floating over
   a ruined city. She had at her command serpents of water.

VII.

Cassandra cannot think of anything to say.
She sits alone in a room too small to stand up in.

You are not asleep with a person, but their whole life.
I reach out my hand in the night, and asleep you hold it.

There is a small barred window full of learning.
Cassandra will recover sooner than she had hoped.

The best way of knowing God is to love many things.
I have not done well, and, sorry, do the same again.

Remember an adult is not three children in an overcoat.
The key to growing up is ...
                         Look, look! A tree! A cloud! Life!

I learn to carry this like precious liquid I must not spill.
Oh my past forgive me. Oh my past I am not ready to let you go.

i only travel when they pay my expenses
that's why i hold it tight this little obol

ACKNOWLEDGEMENTS

Thanks are due to *PN Review*, *Literary Review* and *Poetry London*, where versions of some of these poems first appeared.

I am still benefitting from a prepandemic month spent at Hawthornden Castle, where some of these poems were drafted and considered and conceived.

In-text acknowledgements: phrases that sound like quotations probably are.

Most of my thinking about how some of the more successful poems here should fit together comes from talking about poetry with Sylee Gore.

As always, vital thanks are due to my wife Marian, who is an astute and direct critic. I would also like to thank my children for keeping out of the way at delicate moments.